Blossom

Bloom Where You Are Planted

Dina Ezzeddine

BLOSSOM. Copyright © 2023, 2024 by Dina Ezzeddine.

All rights reserved.

No portion of this book may be reproduced in any form without written permission from the publisher or author, except as permitted by Canada's copyright laws.

This publication is designed to provide accurate and authoritative information in regard to the subject matter covered. It is sold with the understanding that neither the author nor the publisher is engaged in rendering legal, investment, accounting or other professional services.

Cover Images used under license.

Published by: Lulu Publishing, and all eBook platforms.

ISBN: 978-1-0690893-6-6 (softcover)

Blossom
Bloom Where You Are Planted

Contents

1. Roots of Hope
2. Petals of Strength
3. Rain and Renewal
4. Sunlit Paths

Buried Treasure

Beneath the soil of doubt,
your roots spread wide—
hope is a seed
that refuses to hide.

Whisper of the Earth

The ground hums,
"Start here,
right where you are."
Each whisper
is a promise of growth.

Foundation

The ground hums,
"Start here,
right where you are."
Each whisper
is a promise of growth.

Invisible Progress

What blooms above
is only a fraction
of the work done below.

First Green

The first sprout is small,
but in its tiny frame,
there is a world
of potential.

Beneath the Surface

Before a bloom can rise,
it works tirelessly below,
digging into the depths
where no light dares to go.

Roots of Courage

When the storms come,
the roots do not question their strength.
They dig deeper,
clinging to the earth,
holding steadfast
even when the world above
seems to collapse.
Every tree standing tall
once trusted its unseen foundation.

The Forgotten Seed

A seed forgotten
will still grow,
even in the cracks
of yesterday's dreams.

Grounded in Faith

Your roots may not
touch the sky,
but they hold
all the weight of it.

Soft Beginnings

Roots start softly,
fragile as threads,
but they weave a strength
that defies the earth's pull.

You are a masterpiece in progress, a bloom unfolding in its own time. The world may try to measure you against its own rigid standards, but remember this: flowers don't compete with each other to grow. They simply rise, reaching toward the light in their own beautiful, unique ways.

Life's storms may bend your stem, but they will never break the essence of who you are. Every raindrop that falls is nurturing you, every ray of sunlight is a reminder that you deserve to be here, thriving, just as you are.

Stand tall, even in the shadows. Trust that your roots are strong, anchoring you to all the lessons and strength you've gathered along the way. When you bloom, do it unapologetically—wild and free. You don't need permission to thrive. You don't need validation to shine.

You are already enough. You are worthy of love, including the love you give yourself. Bloom where you are standing, and know that even in the smallest moments, you are growing into something extraordinary.

Underneath

You only see the bloom—
never the toil beneath.
Yet the roots remain the reason
for beauty.

Anchor

Roots are anchors—
not to keep you still,
but to help you weather
what's to come.

Unseen Strength

You underestimate
what you cannot see.
Beneath the surface,
strength is woven,
layer by layer,
a network of resolve.
What seems small
is immeasurably vast
when you dare to look closer.

Starting Over

Every fallen leaf
gives way
to a new beginning.

The Ground Below

The earth doesn't judge
where you plant your roots.
It simply gives
what it can.

Life Beneath

There is life beneath the stillness—
a hum of energy
waiting to rise.

Silent Growth

Not all growth is loud;
some roots dig quietly
but deeply.

You are stronger than you realize, more beautiful than you see, and more loved than you know. Trust in your journey, even when the path feels uncertain. Every step you take, every moment you choose to rise, is a testament to your resilience. Embrace yourself fully—your flaws, your strengths, your growth. You are a wild bloom, radiant and free. Keep growing, keep shining, and remember: you are enough, just as you are.

Frayed Edges

Strength isn't perfect,
it's frayed at the edges,
stitched together
by every moment
you didn't quit.

Windswept

The storm shook your petals,
but never your roots.
You are still standing.

Carried Away

Let the wind take
what you don't need.
Your strength
is in what remains.

Worn Petals

Every petal bears a story:
the time the sun kissed it too long,
the night the frost arrived uninvited,
the storm that carried away a piece of it.
Yet it still blooms,
defiant,
radiant,
unafraid of what comes next.

The Bloom Knows

A flower knows
its worth.
Why else would it bloom
just to be seen?

Holding On

Some petals fall,
but others cling,
refusing to let go.

The Strongest Bloom

The strongest bloom
is not the brightest—
it's the one
that rises after every storm.

Weathering

You've weathered storms
that tried to take everything.
Yet here you are,
still standing.

Resilience

Strength is found
not in standing tall,
but in bending
without breaking.

Sunlit Survivor

Each scar on your petals
is proof
that you've faced the light
and lived.

Certainly! Here's a medium-length message filled with encouragement:

It's okay to cry. It's okay to feel sadness, to sit with the weight of your emotions and let the tears flow. Those tears are not a sign of weakness—they are proof that you care, that you feel deeply, that you are human.

But let me remind you of this: even in your moments of sadness, you are amazing. You are strong for carrying the pain, and beautiful for letting it out. There is no shame in breaking; every flower bends in the wind before it straightens again.

So take your time. Feel what you need to feel, but never forget the incredible person you are. You have survived every storm so far, and you are still here, still blooming in your own way. Be gentle with yourself. You are worthy of love, kindness, and the beauty that this life has to offer—even on the hard days.

Petals of Steel

Delicate, they call you—
but they don't know
the strength it takes
to keep blooming
in a world
that tests you
again and again.

The Petal's Choice

A petal can fall,
or it can hold on
until the very end.
Both are choices of strength.

Resilient Beauty

Your petals may not
be perfect,
but they are beautiful
because they endured.

Growth Through Pain

Every petal lost
was a lesson learned.
Every bloom gained
was a triumph earned.

Standing Tall

Strength is not just
in surviving the storm—
it's in standing tall
to face the next.

Unbreakable Bloom

Even the fiercest winds
could not take you.
You are unbreakable.

Thorns and All

Strength does not hide
its imperfections.
It wears them
like armor.

Defiant Blossom

Defiant,
you rose in a garden
that tried to bury you.
Your roots dug deep;
your petals refused to fade.
You are not just a bloom—
you are a testament
to survival.

Defiant, you rose in a garden that tried to bury you. Your roots dug deep; your petals refused to fade. You are not just a bloom— you are a testament to survival.

Gentle Downpour

Rain does not destroy.
It softens,
it nurtures,
it reminds you
to keep growing.

After the Storm

Each droplet clings to you—
proof that you survived.
Proof that you're alive.

Morning Dew

Even the smallest droplets
hold the light.
Every tear,
a moment of clarity.

Rebirth

You aren't starting over;
you're starting again,
stronger,
wiser,
and beautifully renewed.

The Dance of Rain

The rain falls not to drown,
but to cleanse.
Each drop whispers:
"Release.
Let go.
Begin again."
And in the rhythm of its dance,
you find your own.

Healing Waters

Rain falls for the earth,
but it also falls for you—
to soothe,
to heal,
to remind you
that nothing grows
without a little storm.

Washing Away

Every storm washes away
what no longer serves you.

Echoes of the Rain

The rain whispers softly,
"Even the heaviest storms
pass in time."

Flood of Renewal

Sometimes the rain feels endless,
but in its flood,
new life emerges.

Cloudburst

You held it all in—
every ache,
every silent cry.
Then came the cloudburst,
and though it felt like breaking,
it was the beginning
of your renewal.

You deserve to love yourself deeply—not just for who you are now, but for every version of yourself that brought you here. Love the you who stumbled, the you who doubted, and the you who grew despite it all.

You are worthy of kindness, especially your own. Speak gently to yourself, as you would to someone you cherish. Celebrate your wins, no matter how small, and honor your scars, for they are proof of your resilience.

You are more than enough, just as you are. Let self-love bloom within you like the wildflower you've always been—beautiful, untamed, and wholly deserving of the light you seek.

Tears of the Sky

Even the sky cries,
and after its tears fall,
the sun always returns.

Streams of Growth

The rain carves paths
into the earth,
just as your tears
carve paths
toward your growth.

Drenched in Hope

Let the rain drench you
in its truth:
even the hardest storms
are temporary.

Soft Thunder

Even in its roar,
thunder carries
the promise of clarity.

Cleansing Chaos

The storm came to scatter,
to rearrange,
to rebuild.

Puddle Reflections

Rain leaves behind mirrors—
puddles where you can see
what you've become.

Rain Rebirth

Every drop whispers:
"You are ready to bloom again."

Eternal Renewal

No storm is eternal,
and neither is the pain.
The rain does not stay;
it moves on,
and in its wake,
new life springs forth.
So will you.

Never hate yourself. You are human, and mistakes are part of your journey. Always forgive yourself—with every misstep, you are learning, growing, and becoming. Show yourself the same love and compassion you so freely give to others, because you deserve it too.

Golden Hours

No storm is eternal,
and neither is the pain.
The rain does not stay;
it moves on,
and in its wake,
new life springs forth.
So will you.

Breaking Dawn

Every morning is proof
that the night
never wins.

Light Within

You don't need the sun
to glow.
You've carried its light
in your chest
all along.

Paths Unseen

Even the trail-less woods
welcome the brave bloom
that chooses
to create its way.

Chasing the Sun

You are not a shadow,
you are the light that chases the sun.
Even when clouds gather,
your glow remains—
soft,
persistent,
undeniable.

Rays of Strength

The sun's rays touch everything—
even the parts
you think are unworthy.

Stepping Forward

Every step
is a chance
to find the light.

Sunlit Survivor

You survived the storm,
now let the sun
carry you forward.

You've made it this far—through the pages and through your own journey. Remember, no matter where you are planted, you have the power to bloom. Keep growing, keep shining, and never stop believing in the beauty within you.

IN THIS COLLECTION
GRAB YOUR COPY TODAY!

DANCE IN THE RAIN

COFFEE SEASON

THINGS I CAN'T SAY

SEASONS IN BLOOM

AMAZON, BARNES & NOBLE, COLES/INDIGO BOOK STORES & EVERYWHERE!

IN THE SELF-LOVE COLLECTION

GRAB YOUR COPY TODAY!

BLOOM

BLOSSOM

AMAZON, BARNES & NOBLE, COLES/INDIGO BOOK STORES & EVERYWHERE!

CHILDREN'S BOOK COLLECTION

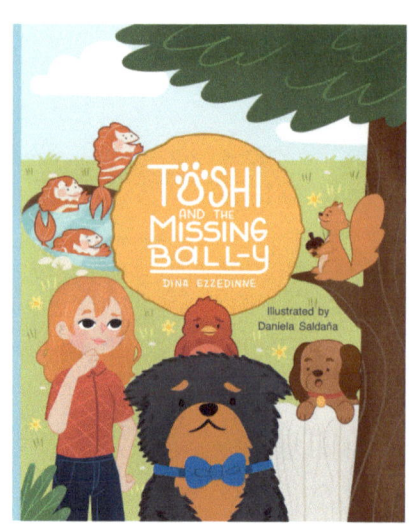

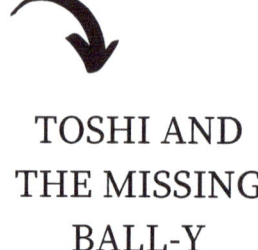

TOSHI AND THE MISSING BALL-Y

I AM LEBANESE

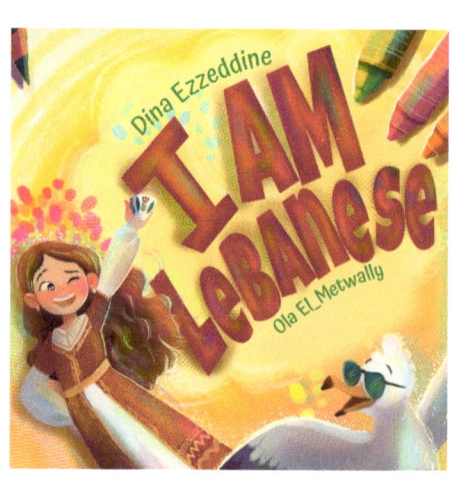

AMAZON, BARNES & NOBLE, COLES/INDIGO BOOK STORES & EVERYWHERE!

A Note on the Author

Dina Ezzeddine is a writer and illustrator from Canada. Dina has a degree in Visual Arts and Design, as well as a Bachelor of Arts degree in English. Dina has written numerous children's book and numerous teen books. This book of poetry is her latest work. You can find more of Dina's upcoming work online!

Find more of Dina's here:
visit Amazon & Barnes & Noble

----

author_illustratordina
aiko10195@gmail.com
missDinaAuthor

LEAVE US A REVIEW!

----

ve us your opinions and thoughts
on any of our works!
herever books are sold!

www.ingramcontent.com/pod-product-compliance
Lightning Source LLC
Chambersburg PA
CBHW041512010526
44118CB00006B/232